Kingdom Files:

Who Was Daniel?

Kingdom Files:

Who Was Daniel?

Matt Koceich

BARBOUR BOOKS
An Imprint of Barbour Publishing, Inc.

Print ISBN 978-1-68322-627-7

eBook Editions:
Adobe Digital Edition (.epub) 978-1-68322-895-0
Kindle and MobiPocket Edition (.prc) 978-1-68322-901-8

Cover design by C. B. Canga
Interior illustration by Patricia Yuste

Published by Barbour Books, an imprint of Barbour Publishing, Inc., 1810 Barbour Drive, Uhrichsville, Ohio 44683, www.barbourbooks.com

Our mission is to inspire the world with the life-changing message of the Bible.

Member of the
Evangelical Christian
Publishers Association

Printed in the United States of America.

06136 0718 CM

Dear Reading Detective,

Welcome to Kingdom Files! You're now a very important part of the Kingdom Files investigation—a series of really cool biographies all found in the Bible. Each case you investigate focuses on an important Bible character and is separated into three sections to make your time fun and interesting. First, you'll find the **Fact File**, which contains key information about a specific Bible character whom God called to do big things for His kingdom. Next, you'll read through an **Action File** that lays out Bible events showing the character inaction. And finally, the **Power File** is where you'll find valuable information and memory verses to help you see how God is work-ing in your life too. Along the way, **Clue Boxes** will offer applications to help you keep track of your thoughts as you make your way through the files. You can also use these sections to record questions you might have along Daniel's journey. Write down any questions, and then ask your parents to get them involved in your quest.

Before you begin, know this: not only did God have plans for the Bible characters you'll read about in the Kingdom Files, but Jeremiah 29:11 says that God has big plans for you too! I pray that *Kingdom Files: Who Was Daniel?* helps you get a bigger picture of God, and that you will see just how much He loves you!

Blessings,

M.K.

Name: **DANIEL**

Occupation: **prophet**

From: **Jerusalem**

Years Active: **605–536 BC**

Kingdom Work: **served as a prophet to the people of Judah, who were being held captive in Babylon**

Mini Timeline:

605 BC
Taken captive to Babylon

586 BC
Jerusalem destroyed

553 BC
Daniel's first vision

536 BC
Daniel's ministry ends

Key Stats:

✦ Stayed committed to God even though times were tough

✦ Did his kingdom work for seventy years in a foreign land

✦ Trusted God with everything

In Training

Times were tough. Life as everyone knew it in Jerusalem was flipped upside down after a foreign king came to town and commanded his troops to take over the land. *Besiege,* actually. That's a fancy word that means to surround a city with soldiers in order to capture it.

Can you imagine? You and your family are taken captive and forced to move

CLUES

Daniel was part of the royal family in Jerusalem and therefore from the line of King David. (Jesus would come from this same line too.) And even though Daniel had his world wrecked, he never used it as an excuse to walk away from God. In fact, he used it to get closer to Him.

far away and obey a new set of rules. Everything you own is taken from you. You have to start life all over again, afraid and uncertain of the future. That's exactly what happened to Daniel.

Daniel was a very smart young man. And even with all his knowledge, Daniel still rested in God's will and not his own. In addition to these admirable qualities, Daniel was also a pro at understanding people's dreams with God's help, and he led an extremely righteous life—always ready to obey the laws of the Lord.

~~~~~~~~~~

The name Daniel means "God has judged." This is very interesting because even though the Babylonians took Daniel and the Israelites captive,

Daniel means:

GOD HAS JUDGED

God had already mapped out their victory. God had big plans for Daniel. Daniel was in captivity for seventy years, and the great prophet used every one of those years to do bold kingdom work for God's glory.

Our investigation into the life of Daniel begins with an epic invasion. Daniel lived in Jerusalem when the Babylonian king Nebuchadnezzar invaded.

Daniel plus countless other Jewish people were forced from their homes and made to travel nearly a thousand miles to the city of Babylon. All of the world's nations bowed down to Nebuchadnezzar. That's a pretty powerful position to hold! But this earthly kingdom, despite its power and influence, would be no match for God's glorious kingdom.

In captivity, Daniel served under the rule of four different kings. Kings rule for only a short time and then they are gone, but God's kingdom lasts forever!

Daniel was carried away from everything he knew and taken to a strange land with a foreign language and many different customs. This new culture was overwhelming, but Daniel made the most of a truly bad situation.

Once Daniel arrived in Babylon, the king ordered him to be brought into his service. Now, Daniel wasn't called by name, but he did fit the description that Nebuchadnezzar was looking for: young, physically fit, handsome, smart, and good at learning new things. There were three other young men who were named in Daniel's story—Hananiah, Mishael, and Azariah. If you're familiar with this story, you might remember that they were given new names—Shadrach, Meshach, and Abednego (see Daniel 1:6).

For the first three years in Babylon, Daniel and his three new friends were given a new education. They were expected to learn the language and

literature of the new culture. And after three years of training, the young men would then be ready to be in the service of the king. In addition to the good education they would receive, the king also decided to share his food, giving Daniel and the students daily meals and wine from his table.

But Daniel, being a child of God, realized that this went against his desire to respect God and His laws. So Daniel asked an official if they could have something else to eat.

This stressed out the official because he was

afraid that if Daniel and the other young men didn't eat the good food from the king, they would become unhealthy. Daniel acted in faith and requested that the official let them do a test. Daniel and his friends would eat only vegetables and drink only water for ten days and then be compared to the others who were eating from the king's table. The Bible says that God caused the official to show Daniel favor and thus allowed the challenge.

Remember that God had big plans for Daniel.

God was with Daniel, and so when the ten days were over, Daniel and company looked "healthier and better nourished than any of the young men who ate the royal food" (1:15). After that, Daniel and the others were allowed to eat their vegetables and drink water so they would not go against God's instructions for their lives.

The young men continued on in their studies, but it was God who gave them "knowledge and understanding of all kinds of literature and learning" (1:17). God gave them an abundance of what they

needed to do His kingdom work. When God blesses, He does it abundantly. And when Daniel and his three friends were presented to the king,

Nebuchadnezzar could find no one else who was equal to them. The Bible says they were "ten times better than all the magicians and enchanters in his whole kingdom" (1:20). That's some pretty powerful God-sized training!

A Very Interesting Dream

While Daniel's training was going on, the king was beginning to have some problems of his own. The Bible says "His mind was troubled and he could not sleep" (2:1). The King had many dreams, and they were so unbelievable that he couldn't figure out what they meant. Nebuchadnezzar called in some people to help him figure things out. He summoned magicians and enchanters as well as sorcerers and astrologers who were put together on his "dream team."

Imagine this group standing before the king. They were looking at each other and wondering what job they were about to be given by the highest authority in the land. The king told them that he'd had dreams, but one in particular was especially bothering him because he had no clue what it meant. The group of astrologers stepped forward and said that if the king would tell them the dream, they would surely be able to interpret it for him.

But instead of describing his dream, the king told the astrologers that they must figure out what his dream was as well as what it meant. And if they couldn't, they would lose their lives and all of their houses would be "turned into piles of rubble" (2:5). The king was surely stressed out at this point. He then told the men that if they were able to tell him the dream and interpret it correctly, they would receive gifts and high honors.

The reply? Again, the group said that all they needed was for the king to tell them the details of the dream, and then they would be glad to explain its meaning. But the king wasn't convinced. He thought they were stalling. He reminded them that there was going to be a penalty if they couldn't come up with an answer. They said, "There is no one on earth who can do what the king asks!" (2:10). The men said that only the "gods" could tell the king what he wanted to know.

Nebuchadnezzar became so furious that he ordered all the wise men in the entire land to be put to death. And that included Daniel and his friends!

When the king's guard met with Daniel, he was in for quite a surprise. Daniel boldly asked why the king would make such an irrational decision just because the wise

CLUES

Daniel and his friends were taken against their will and made to travel a very great distance where they had to start life all over again in a new culture. But God never left Daniel's side. Remember that God allowed the official to grant Daniel's request for the special diet. With the king's dream, God was setting things up so He could use Daniel in a mighty way for His kingdom plans.

men couldn't tell what his dream entailed. After the man explained the situation, Daniel went directly to the king himself. Talk about courage! Daniel asked for time to be able to interpret the

king's dream, and by God's mercy, the king agreed.

Daniel urged his friends to join him in pleading for mercy from God and to ask God for help. Daniel prayed first. Even though his life and the lives of his three friends were on the line, Daniel didn't panic. He prayed and talked to God. He asked God for help, and he was about to get it in a huge way.

That night while Daniel was asleep, God gave him a vision that outlined the king's dream and the meaning of it as well. When Daniel woke up, he didn't waste a single minute. He prayed again and lifted up praise to thank God for what He did.

Daniel's praise listed some of God's attributes that can help us better understand who God really is. Daniel started off by saying that the name of God should be praised forever. His name is worthy of glory and honor. God is wise and powerful. God changes the times and seasons. He raises up kings and takes them off thrones. He is a wisdom giver.

"Light dwells with him" (2:22). Then Daniel said that God gave him wisdom and power.

Armed with knowledge and answers, Daniel raced to the king's official and told him to stop getting rid of the wise men. God literally used Daniel to

CLUES

Think about it: God gives who He is. So when we feel unloved, God gives us His real love because that's who He is! If we feel discouraged, God gives courage because that's who He is!

save lives, physically and spiritually. The official took Daniel to the king. It was showtime!

The king asked Daniel the same thing he had asked his wise men; and Daniel had a similar, yet completely, different reply. He, like the men earlier, said that no one could do what the king was asking. But unlike the wise men, Daniel said there is a "God in heaven who reveals mysteries" (2:28).

First, Daniel told the king that his dream was about things to come. Daniel made it clear that he didn't get this information because he was better than anybody else, but rather because God would allow Nebuchadnezzar to understand the dream. Remember that this is the same king who had captured Daniel and his friends and so many more people. This is the same king who had seized Jerusalem. Why would Daniel or God want to help him?

The king had dreamed of a huge statue. The head of the statue was made of gold, its chest and arms were silver, its stomach and thighs were made of bronze, its legs were iron, while the feet were a mixture of iron and baked clay. (It was a really weird dream!)

Daniel then told the king that he saw a rock come and smash the statue's feet, which caused the whole statue to crumble into a million pieces.

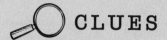
The wind came and blew all the pieces away so that no one would ever know the statue even existed. And in the final part of the king's dream, the rock grew up to become "a huge mountain" that "filled the whole earth" (2:35).

Then Daniel began to explain the meaning of the king's dream. Daniel respectfully said that Nebuchadnezzar was the king of kings. In other words, he was the biggest guy on the block. Again, Daniel added that the king was where he was because God had given all of it to him. Everyone in the world at that time came under the ruling power of the king. King Nebuchadnezzar was the head of gold. This all sounded good to the king—at least for a moment.

Daniel went on to explain that the rest of the statue represented other kingdoms that would rise up and take Babylon's place. And during their reigns, God would set up a kingdom "that will never be destroyed, nor will it be left to another people. It will crush all those kingdoms and bring them to an end, but it will itself endure forever" (2:44).

Whoa! That's some heavy interpreting that Daniel pulled off all because God was there to help him.

So what do you think the king would do with this new information? The Bible says he fell prostrate on the ground before Daniel to honor him. He also put Daniel in a high place and let him rule over all of Babylon. He gave Daniel a ton of gifts, put him in charge of all the wise men, and appointed his friends Shadrach, Meshach, and Abednego to become administrators to help Daniel.

Things began to look up for the prophet.

3

The Golden Statue

With God's help, Daniel stepped
up and delivered exactly what
the king needed to hear. After
learning what his strange dream
meant, it seemed likely that
Nebuchadnezzar would wake
up and realize that his kingdom
wasn't going to last forever. But
instead, he took his dream and
used it as a blueprint to create
a massive golden statue—
ninety feet tall by nine feet
wide, to be exact. And unlike the
dream, the king called for the
whole statue to be made of gold.

He had it built out on the "plain of Dura in the province of Babylon" (3:1). For some reason, the king didn't care about God, even though he had just experienced the dream interpretation with Daniel. And King Nebuchadnezzar summoned all of his leaders from across the empire to the unveiling ceremony.

After all the people had gathered in front of the idol, a herald gave the order that when the musicians started playing their instruments, everyone was to "fall down and worship the image" (3:5). If a person refused, they would be thrown into a fiery furnace so big that grown men could walk in it. Archaeologists believe the main use of this furnace was to make bricks.

When the music started, everyone on the plain fell down and worshipped the golden statue. But remember Daniel's three friends,

Shadrach, Meshach, and Abednego? Well, apparently someone caught them not bowing down and worshipping the idol, and this news was immediately reported to the king. These men loved God and had made a commitment not to be disrespectful and not to worship anything but Him.

When he heard the news, the king became "furious with rage" (3:13) and called for the three men to be brought before him. Nebuchadnezzar asked them if the report was true, and they said it was. The king didn't wait for them to explain. He just continued on and repeated the command that they were to bow down to the statue when the music started, and said that it would be good for them to obey. Then the king asked what god would save them from the fire if they didn't bow down.

They said, "We do not need to defend ourselves

before you in this matter. If we are thrown into the blazing furnace, the God we serve is able to deliver us from it" (3:16–17). They even said that if God chose not to save them from the flames, still they would never worship the king's golden idol.

The king grew even more furious than before. *How dare these three men disobey me?* he thought. So Nebuchadnezzar ordered the oven to be heated up seven times hotter than normal. And if that wasn't enough, he also ordered some of his strongest soldiers to tie the men up. The king didn't want to leave any room for error.

But as the soldiers took the men to the furnace, the flames killed the soldiers but not Daniel's

three friends. The Bible says that even though
they fell into the fire, they were not burned!

And when the king looked into the furnace,
he couldn't believe his eyes! Not only were the
three men still alive, despite the raging flames,
but there was a fourth man in the oven with
them! The fourth man was "unbound and

unharmed" and looked like "a son of the gods" (3:25). It's not clear whether it was an angel or Jesus in the furnace with them, but God had made a way for the men to be saved.

The king called for the men to come out of the furnace. All the officials who had bowed down to the statue were now gathered around and stared in amazement. The fire had not "harmed their bodies, nor was a hair of their heads singed; their robes were not scorched, and there was no smell of fire on them" (3:27).

God had saved His servants! The king was spellbound. He proclaimed that God should be honored among all the nations. Nebuchadnezzar wasn't done with his idol worship, though. He was just telling the world that Daniel's God was powerful and that no one should speak against Him. Either way, the king promoted Daniel's three friends to high positions within the province of Babylon.

More Dreams and New Kings

The king was really getting some good nights of sleep, because right after the fiery furnace drama, he was back to having strange dreams. His next

dream was about an enormous tree. Nebuchad-nezzar watched as the tree grew very tall and very strong. It grew and grew until it touched the sky and could be seen from all the ends of the earth. "Its leaves were beautiful, its fruit abundant, and on it was food for all" (4:12). Wild animals found shelter under the tree, and many birds made homes in its branches. The tree provided food for all the creatures.

In the next part of the dream, the king saw a messenger come down from heaven who issued an order for the tree to be cut down and trimmed of its branches, stripped of all its leaves, and the fruit thrown out in every direction. The tree could no longer be a home for all the wild animals.

The only things that were to remain were the stump and roots. Also, the dreamer was to live with the animals.

The king called for Daniel to do his job and offer a meaning for this new dream. But Daniel was nervous because he soon realized that the dream wasn't about the king's enemies. The dream was about the king himself! Daniel explained all the positives first—the king was great, and his rules extended all the way to the ends of the earth. But then Daniel told the king that he would be taken away from his subjects and would be made to eat the grass of the fields just like an ox. The king would stay this way until he acknowledged that God was the true sovereign king.

It took awhile for the dream to be fulfilled, but a year later the king was walking on the roof of his palace, making comments about how all of what he could see came by the work of his hands. As soon as he spoke these words, the Bible says he heard a voice call down from heaven and tell Nebuchadnezzar that his authority was being pulled from him, and he was about to be sent out to live with wild animals for seven years! His hair and nails

grew so long the king started to look like a wild animal himself. He even began to lose his mind.

But at the end of the seven years, the king lifted his eyes to heaven, and then his sanity was restored. King Nebuchadnezzar began to praise God and give Him glory. He said that God's "dominion is an eternal dominion" and "his kingdom endures from generation to generation" (4:34). Then he got his throne back and admitted that he was an even greater king than before. Nebuchadnezzar said that God humbles the prideful.

One day later, the king had stepped down and his son, Belshazzar, became the new king. He had a big dinner party with a thousand guests. During the festivities, the new king ordered the gold and silver goblets that his father had taken from the temple in Jerusalem be brought in so they could drink from them. As they were drinking from them, the Bible says they began praising the gods of gold, silver, bronze, iron, wood, and stone.

As this was going on, the fingers of a hand appeared and began writing on one of the palace walls! The king became afraid. "His legs became weak and his knees were knocking" (5:6). Then, just like his father before him, Belshazzar called in all his people to see if they could tell him what it meant. He offered them a purple robe and a gold chain and even a very high position of authority. But no one could explain what the writing on the wall meant.

At this point, the queen came in and said not to worry because there was a man named Daniel in the kingdom who could help. She relayed everything that Daniel did to help Nebuchadnezzar and claimed that Daniel could help the new king too.

So Daniel was brought in before the king and offered the gifts for a correct interpretation. Daniel told the king to keep the gifts and give them to someone else but that he would help explain the writing.

The first thing Daniel did was remind Belshazzar all about his father's experiences on the throne. He talked about how his heart became prideful and he was forced to live like a wild animal until he came to the place where he acknowledged God as the sovereign ruler of all the earth. Then Daniel said that Belshazzar knew all this and still didn't humble himself. He said that God holds the king's life in his hands and that he was acting very disrespectful to God by praising the other gods.

And then Daniel spoke about the writing:
MENE, MENE, TEKEL, UPHARSIN.

He said, "*Mene:* [means] God has numbered the days of your reign and brought it to an end. *Tekel:* [means] You have been weighed on the scales and found wanting" (5:26–27). "Found wanting" means that people weren't living like they should and needed to change their behavior. Daniel went on, "*Peres:* [means] Your kingdom is divided and given to the Medes and Persians" (v. 28).

The king was satisfied with Daniel's interpretation and gave him a purple royal robe, a really nice gold chain, and a very important job. Daniel was promoted to third highest ruler in the kingdom! He didn't do all of the interpreting for the gifts, but since Daniel loved to stay connected with God, his words to the new king came from his desire to see more people know God.

That very night the king's life was taken by the enemy, and a man named Darius the Mede took over the kingdom.

Lions!

One of the first things the new king did was appoint new mini-rulers throughout the land, called satraps, to make sure his kingdom would be protected. Then Darius appointed three administrators to look over the satraps—one of them was Daniel. In fact, Daniel was so respected that the new king wanted to put him in charge of the whole kingdom.

The other administrators and rulers didn't like this at all and immediately tried to find ways to get Daniel kicked out. But they had a big problem because Daniel was "trustworthy and neither corrupt nor negligent" (6:4).

The men had to get creative. So they decided to go to the king and recommend that he come up with a new law. The new law would make it a crime to pray to anyone except the king for a month! And the punishment for the "crime"? Getting thrown into the lions' den! The king listened to the men and put the new law in writing.

When Daniel heard of this new law, he went home and prayed like he always did, giving thanks to God. Then men followed Daniel and caught him praying to God for help. They quickly went back to the king and told him that Daniel had disobeyed the law. The king cared for Daniel, and he tried to save him from the punishment of the lions' den.

The men reminded the king that a law is a law, so King Darius ordered Daniel be sent to the lions' den. The king said to Daniel, "May your God, whom you serve continually, rescue you!" (6:16). Then the king had a stone rolled in front of the den opening so Daniel couldn't escape. He returned to the palace worried about Daniel. He couldn't eat or sleep.

As soon as the sun came up the next morning, the king hurried to the lions' den. As he got close, the king called out to Daniel, asking if God was able to save him. Here's what Daniel said: "My God sent his angel, and he shut the mouths of the lions. They have not hurt me, because I was found innocent in his sight. Nor have I ever done any wrong before you" (6:22). The king was so excited. He had

Daniel lifted from the pit and saw that not even a scratch was on him.

The king ordered the men who had tried to get Daniel in trouble and their families to be thrown to the lions. And then he wrote a decree to all the people living around the world. The king wanted everyone to honor God. He wrote: "For he is the living God and he endures forever; his kingdom will not be destroyed, his dominion will never end. He rescues and he saves; he performs signs and wonders in the heavens and on the earth" (6:26–27).

6

A Dream of Four Beasts!

While Daniel was busy interpreting the dreams of kings, he himself was also having dreams. These can be very confusing and hard to understand, but the most important thing to remember is that God gave Daniel these dreams to give the people hope.

One dream that Daniel had was about four big beasts. These beasts represented four empires that each had control over the land that God's people lived in.

The dream began with Daniel standing on a beach, and the wind stirred up the waters. And then creatures emerged from the sea. The first beast to appear looked like a lion but had wings like an eagle. As Daniel continued to watch, the lion was lifted up as the wings were removed. The

creature stood on its two feet like a man, and Daniel saw a man's heart was given to the lion.

CLUES

The Babylonian Empire was the lion, and the eagle represented the speed with which King Nebuchadnezzar conquered the lands to build his kingdom. The man's heart represented how the mighty empire became weak and was a sign that it would fail.

The next beast that appeared looked like a bear. Daniel saw three ribs in its mouth. A voice commanded the bear to eat until it was satisfied. The third creature that appeared before Daniel resembled a leopard. It had four wings on its back. This animal had four heads and

"was given authority to rule" (7:6). The last creature appeared at night and was very powerful. Daniel described it as "terrifying and frightening" (v. 7). It had large teeth made of iron, and it destroyed everything in sight. It was different than all the other beasts and had ten horns.

CLUES

The beast that looked like a bear represented the Persian Empire, and the ribs symbolized the lands that it had conquered.

All of these creatures were eventually destroyed. Daniel recorded these dreams as a way to give the people of God hope. He was saying that we may face hard times now, but as a part of God's kingdom, we cannot be defeated!

The dream ended with Daniel seeing a figure he called one "like a son of man, coming with the clouds of heaven.... He was given authority, glory and sovereign power" (7:13–14). Daniel asked someone next to him for help in understanding the dream. This was a reference to Jesus who came from

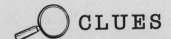

CLUES

The third beast represented the Greek Empire. This empire was greater than the "lion" in that it had four wings instead of the lion's two. The four heads represented the four captains who each received a portion of the empire after Alexander the Great died.

above, while the beasts came from below. The beasts represented kings who ruled for a short while, but God's children would receive the kingdom and live with Him forever in heaven. And for us today, this means, as we will see, that even though bad things happen, Jesus is our ultimate King, and He has already won the battle for our hearts.

 CLUES

Scholars believe the last creature symbolized either Rome or Syria. Both were empires and both brought suffering upon the people of God. The large teeth made of iron refer to the armies and the bad things they did. Daniel said that at this point, a small horn came up between them. It had a mouth and eyes and started to speak. Then the beast was destroyed and thrown into a fire, while the other three creatures were allowed to live for a while longer.

Daniel's Prayer

After his dreams, Daniel began thinking about how the city of Jerusalem would be destroyed and how the hard times would last seventy years. He was sad and went to the Lord in prayer. Daniel fasted and wore sackcloth too. Sackcloth was a rough material made from goat's hair—and it wasn't comfortable. In Bible times, people wore sackcloth as a sign of being sorry for something.

Daniel began his prayer by telling God that He was great and awesome and kept His promises. He said that God loves those who love Him and keep His commandments. Then Daniel admitted that his people had sinned. He said that everyone had rebelled and turned away from God's laws.

Daniel continued to pray, telling God that He

is righteous, but everyone is covered in shame. Daniel said that God is merciful and forgiving. Daniel cried out for God to hear his plea for help. "We do not make requests of you because we are righteous, but because of your great mercy" (9:18). Daniel's prayer turned his heart to God's as he begged God to help.

While Daniel was offering up this prayer, the angel Gabriel came to him again with a message of "seventy sevens." Gabriel told Daniel that while he was praying, word traveled out, and Gabriel received a message that Daniel was praying and went to him. Gabriel said, "Seventy 'sevens' are decreed for your people and your holy city to finish transgression, to put an end to sin, to atone for wickedness, to bring in everlasting righteousness, to seal up vision and prophecy and to anoint the Most Holy Place" (9:24).

The people ended their sinful ways, asked

forgiveness, returned to Jerusalem, and began again. The important part of this message is that Jesus is mentioned as the "Anointed One" (9:26). The message says He will be put to death and have nothing, but that in the end, His eternal and perfect kingdom will come.

Then Daniel had another vision of a man wearing linen and a belt of gold. His body was like topaz and his face like lightning. His eyes were like flaming torches, his arms and legs were like bronze, and his voice sounded like a great crowd. Daniel was learning that there were battles going on behind the scenes in unseen places. Through it all, God was working out His plans to help the people get back to their homeland in Israel.

More Visions of Kings

Daniel continued to have visions that helped him understand God's plan for His people. Daniel learned that there would be kings who would try to harm the Jewish people.

Daniel also learned about the "end times." Daniel heard about the great angel Michael who will rise up and protect God's people. The prophet was also told that believers will have everlasting life with God, but unbelievers will go to a separate place where they experience everlasting "shame…and contempt" (12:2). Daniel also learned that "those who are

CLUES

There will be difficult days, but in the end, Jesus is the victorious King who will save His people.

wise will shine like the brightness of the heavens, and those who lead many to righteousness, like the stars for ever and ever" (12:3).

There were parts of Daniel's visions that he did not completely understand, but he was told by the messenger, "Go your way till the end. You will rest, and then at the end of the days you will rise to receive your allotted inheritance" (12:13). That is how Daniel's story, as recorded in the Bible, ends. It ends on a promise, that one day God would take Daniel home to heaven, and while Daniel waited for that day, he would have peace knowing that God is sovereign and would continue to take care of him.

9

Now that we've investigated the life of Daniel, it's time to think about some lessons we can learn from his story. A lot of Daniel's kingdom work involved using his wisdom to help the very people who held him captive. One of the common themes of Daniel's story is relying on God and staying connected to Him in many different ways. Daniel talked to God about everything, and he always listened to God's instructions. And not only did he listen, but he acted on what he knew was God's desire for his life.

Daniel's story was filled with stresses and successes. He had days when he wasn't sure what was going to happen to him and other days when he could see God at work. Whatever came his way, good or bad, Daniel stood up for God, because that was how he knew life should be lived—standing up for God, because that's what God deserves.

From the start, when Daniel and his people were taken hundreds of miles away to captivity, and until the end of his seventy years of ministry, the prophet took each step with full trust in God and His Word. Daniel didn't allow the day's events to control his view of God. Daniel didn't let his circumstances determine his feelings. Trusting his Creator to know what was best for his life took Daniel further than he ever could have gone if he had doubted.

Daniel learned how to trust God and be faithful. He kept God number one in his life.

Daniel didn't let fear of the unknown dictate his actions or moods. He persevered in a foreign place for seven decades because of his unfaltering faith in God. Daniel persevered because he knew with all his heart that God is in control of everything. God made everything. He is Lord of all, stronger than any force of evil and giver of every blessing. Daniel knew life made sense when he followed God instead of running out ahead of Him.

God also teaches us through Daniel's life that He has a purpose for everything. Life won't always be perfect and stress-free. And life won't always be the same for everyone. God makes His children special and doesn't want them to give up or compare their lives to the lives of other believers. God has a unique and special plan for each one of His children!

Daniel learned along the way that God is a mighty protector. He goes before us and isn't taken off guard by the hard things that come our way. He knows everything we're going through. And for everything you experience, God will use you to do great things for His kingdom and glory.

Now let's look at each one of these valuable lessons individually and some memory verses that will help plant God's truth in our hearts.

Power-Up #1:

MAKE PRAYER A HABIT.

Daniel's story is filled with times when he prayed. Making the right choices and reading the Bible are both very important, but prayer is like the glue that connects us to God. By using Daniel's prayers as examples, we can see that prayer isn't just asking God for things, but praising Him for who He is and what He's done for us. Whatever kind

of day you're having, tell God all about it.
Sharing your feelings will help keep things on
the right track. Talking to God and making
prayer a habit will help you know that, no
matter what, God is right there listening.

MEMORY VERSE: Be joyful in hope, patient
in affliction, faithful in prayer.
Romans 12:12

Power-Up #2:
STAND UP FOR GOD.

Daniel stood strong for his heavenly Father. In the beginning of his story, Daniel had to make a very difficult decision about the kind of food he was going to eat. When he was offered food from the king's table, Daniel was tempted to change his ways and start heading down a path that would have him relying on the king's gifts. But Daniel knew better. As hard as it might have been, Daniel decided to rely on God instead. He had courage to tell the king's official that he wanted only vegetables and water. He wasn't worried about sounding ungrateful. Daniel only wanted to make sure the people he came in contact with knew that God was worth standing up for.

MEMORY VERSE: It is for freedom that Christ has set us free. Stand firm, then, and do not let yourselves be burdened again by a yoke of slavery. Galatians 5:1

Power-Up #3:
TRUST GOD.

When Daniel and his friends were taken captive, their future was uncertain. There were days when Daniel surely wondered what God's plan was in all of it. But through it all, Daniel continued to trust in God. He would end up ministering in his place of captivity for seventy years! At some point, Daniel knew in his heart that the kingdom work God had for him meant staying in the foreign land. Trusting in God wasn't easy. Remember,

Daniel trusted God and still wound up in a den of hungry lions. The important thing to know is that God made you special, and He won't let you go. He has a plan and knows what's best for you. Trust Him more and more as you grow in your faith and get closer to Him.

MEMORY VERSE: The LORD is my strength and my shield; my heart trusts in him, and he helps me. My heart leaps for joy, and with my song I praise him.
Psalm 28:7

Power-Up #4:
REMAIN FAITHFUL.

Daniel stayed connected to God through every trial because he knew that God cared about him. Daniel knew that God would be there for him through everything life would bring. Lives were changed because Daniel had faith in God's love and power. Whether it was food or prayer time, Daniel made it a priority to put God first. Being faithful to God means we pray for wisdom and strength to read our Bibles and let Him guide us in everything we do.

MEMORY VERSE: My eyes will be on the faithful in the land, that they may dwell with me. Psalm 101:6

Power-Up #5:
GOD IS IN CONTROL.

Daniel could have easily given in to fear when he was taken captive. He could have quickly decided to trust in himself and all the things he could see with his eyes. Daniel would have felt good too. Remember, the king offered him the best food and a comfortable life, but Daniel wanted something better. Daniel wanted a relationship with his Creator. For Daniel, God wasn't some unseen force but a Father and Friend. Daniel knew God's grace was enough to get him through every situation. God kept proving Himself faithful to Daniel, which made it easy for Daniel to constantly trust that God was in control of his life.

MEMORY VERSE: "So do not fear, for I am with you; do not be dismayed, for I am your God. I will strengthen you and help you; I will uphold you with my righteous right hand." Isaiah 41:10

Power-Up #6:

GOD HAS A PURPOSE.

One of the inspirational traits of Daniel's character was his ability to always trust that God knows what He's doing. From the beginning, Daniel acted on faith, knowing that God had plans for his life. Daniel also knew that there was a very real enemy (the devil) trying to throw Daniel off track. He knew the enemy wanted to keep Daniel's eyes off God and on his situation. But Daniel stayed on the path God had for him, not wishing he was someplace else doing some other work. He trusted God's purposes, and he kept his heart and mind in God's truth.

MEMORY VERSE: "For I know the plans I have for you," declares the Lord, "plans to prosper you and not to harm you, plans to give you hope and a future." Jeremiah 29:11

Power-Up #7:
DON'T QUIT.

Daniel knew how to keep going for God. He knew how to persevere through the tough times. He relied on God's unstoppable love as he ministered to the kings in Babylon. Daniel didn't give up on God, because he knew that God would never give up on him. Daniel kept his daily faith because he knew God is a promise keeper. Daniel always took God at His word and was blessed because of it.

MEMORY VERSE: Let us not become weary in doing good, for at the proper time we will reap a harvest if we do not give up. Galatians 6:9

Power-Up #8:

GOD PROTECTS.

Daniel's kingdom work teaches us that he lived and moved under God's protection. From the beginning, when his city was invaded, Daniel was protected by God. God wasn't taken by surprise when Nebuchadnezzar's men ransacked Jerusalem. God had Daniel covered both then and during the journey to Babylon. God continued to protect Daniel as he received an education. And when Nebuchadnezzar made everyone bow down to his gigantic statue, Daniel's friends refused to bow down, knowing God would protect them too. Daniel didn't worry about the results, because he was confident that God was his strength and shield.

MEMORY VERSE: But the Lord is faithful, and he will strengthen you and protect you from the evil one. 2 Thessalonians 3:3

Power-Up #9:
GOD KNOWS.

Daniel didn't let his circumstances determine his faith. He understood that God had a plan for his life and that nothing would happen to him without God knowing about it. God was with Daniel before he was taken into captivity, and He remained with him every moment after. When we really believe that God knows everything we're going through, then we can live boldly for Him.

When we trust that God sees and feels all our joy and all of our sorrows, we find true comfort. God made you and knows you, and He doesn't make mistakes, so follow Him always.

MEMORY VERSE: Great is our Lord and mighty in power; his understanding has no limit. Psalm 147:5

Power-Up #10:
GOD WILL USE YOU.

The same great and loving God who made the universe carefully and lovingly made you! Believe the truth that He loves you very much and has great things planned for your life. Daniel's life is an example that God's plans and our plans might be totally different. So, like Daniel, we just have to be available for God to use us for His kingdom and His glory.

If we get into the habit of praying and asking God for His guidance, then we will step out in faith and leave the results up to Him. God will use you for His glory because He cares about you.

MEMORY VERSE: For it is God who works in you to will and to act in order to fulfill his good purpose. Philippians 2:13

Matt Koceich is a husband,

father, and public school teacher.

He and his family live in Texas.

Notes

_____

_____

_____

_____

_____

_____

_____

_____

_____

_____

_____

_____

_____

Notes

Collect Them All!

Kingdom Files: Who Is Jesus?

This biblically accurate biography explores the life of Jesus while drawing readers into a fascinating time and place as they learn about the One who gave sight to the blind, made the lame to walk, raised people from the dead, and who died so that we might live.

Paperback / 978-1-68322-626-0 / $4.99

Kingdom Files: Who Was Esther?

This biblically accurate biography explores the life of Esther while drawing readers into a fascinating time and place as they learn about the beautiful Queen of Persia who hid her Jewish heritage from the king and ultimately risked her life to save her people.

Paperback / 978-1-68322-629-1 / $4.99

Kingdom Files: Who Was David?

This biblically accurate biography explores the life of David while drawing readers into a fascinating time and place as they learn about the shepherd boy turned king who played a harp and slayed a giant with a stone and a sling.

Paperback / 978-1-68322-628-4 / $4.99

Kingdom Files: Who Was Jonah?

This biblically accurate biography explores the life of Jonah while drawing readers into a fascinating time and place as they learn about the reluctant prophet who said "no" to God, was tossed overboard during a storm, and swallowed by a giant fish.

Paperback / 978-1-68322-630-7 / $4.99

Kingdom Files: Who Was Mary, Mother of Jesus?

This biblically accurate biography explores the life of Mary while drawing readers into a fascinating time and place as they learn about the courageous young teenager who said "yes" to God and ultimately gave birth to the Savior of the world.

Paperback / 978-1-68322-631-4 / $4.99